ORANGE GROVE RD
The House Where My Nightmares Began

written by
Cathy

Copyright © Cathy 2024

All rights reserved. No part of this publication may be reproduced, distributed, or transmitted in any form or by any means, including photocopying, recording, or other electronic or mechanical methods, without the prior written permission of the publisher, except in the case of brief quotations embodied in critical reviews and certain other non-commercial uses permitted by copyright law.

✽ greenhill

https://greenhillpublishing.com.au/

Cathy (author)
Orange Grove Rd
ISBN 978-1-923156-22-1
MEMOIR

Typeset Calluna Regular 11/18
Cover and book design by Green Hill Publishing

To my husband who has been my love and my best friend.
You have been my rock through all the adventures in our life, including bringing up our beautiful children.

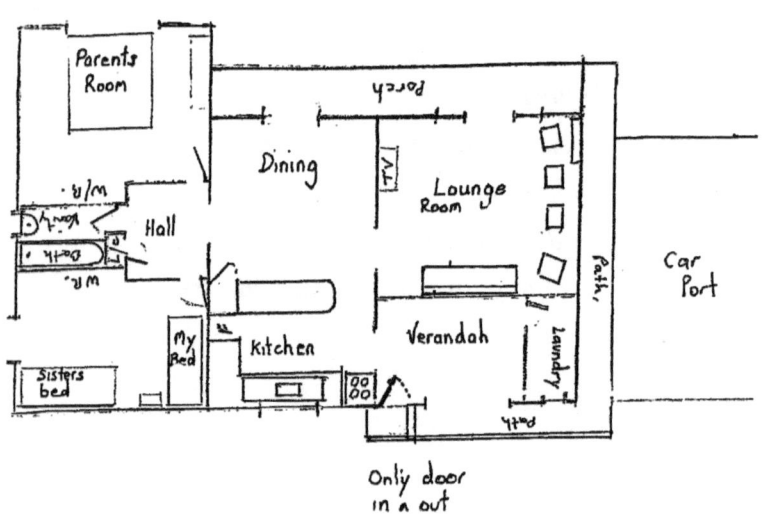

IT MUST HAVE BEEN the winter months in 1967.

It was the year I turned 13 and I clearly remember I was wearing a pale yellow, lacy jumper, which my mother had hand knitted and a pleated tartan skirt, mainly red in colour. They were my best clothes. I was going to a friend's birthday party. I never had a Birthday party myself and I don't think I attended many, but I remember this one, and I remember this day clearly! My friend Betty (the birthday girl) only lived at the bottom of the hill, so I was allowed to attend. It was close enough to walk. You see Mum didn't drive back in those days and Dad was always at work. I had done my hair myself, two pig-tails, but Mum was quick to roll her eyes to show her disapproval of my styling. I don't remember what was occupying Mum that morning as she always did our hair, always the same, pulled back tightly in one high ponytail. At night she would always wrap that ponytail up in a rag or old stocking. We slept with this rigid totally stiff thing on the back of our heads every night, no way where we allowed to wear our hair out. Anyhow, I thought I looked great, it was almost time to set off for the party. I remember how excited I felt going out the back door of the small white fibro house we rented since I was about nine, but those good feelings were about to change. My entire world, as I knew it, was about to crumble. The traumatic scenes of that day and the years that followed are deep in my memory. Within the next few minutes before that walk to the party, I would witness the beginning of a nightmare that would stay with me for the rest of my life.

As I walked out the back door with my sister, a small parcel in my hand, my father rushed past us, not even acknowledging us in our party clothes. My eyes followed him, his face was so angry. He closed the door behind him, well actually he slammed it. I was stopped in my tracks. I could hear his angry voice yelling at mum. As I looked through the gap between the blind and the window edge, I saw my father grab my mother around the throat, push her up against the wall on the back verandah and start hitting her. My ears did not take in one word, but I could hear the rage in my father's voice. My eyes were taking in everything, as time stood still. Suddenly I was standing back inside that door, just staring. Dad turned quickly and I hardly recognised him, his face was so full of rage. He yelled at me go, 'go off to wherever you were going' and mum echoed 'go, get out.' I don't remember the walk down the hill, but I do remember not a word was said. I know I was not sure I could believe my eyes. I didn't have any words that went with the scene to know if it, actually happened. I don't remember anything about the party I was so excited about, but I know I was there, I was given a photo.

Photo 1. The party

As the weeks went by, the atmosphere in our family home was much the same as it had always been. As far as I could see the only thing that was different was me and the way I relived what I had seen and puzzled over the violence. You see my parents rarely spoke quietly. They snapped and sneered at each other never showing affection, you know holding hands or cuddling. Yelling was a normal part of our family life, so I guess for some time, I thought other parents spoke to each other in the same tones, but I knew, that, that Saturday afternoon's violence was not part of my everyday life, and I could not talk to anyone!

Before this Saturday when life changed, my memories, of days out as a family, are clear. There was places and family members my dad would take us. Great Uncle Norm and auntie Glad, was one. They had a farm, can't remember where, but it was the other side of Sydney. Also, Great auntie Gert and her husband George, who lived at Anna Bay, to get there we would drive to Newcastle line up for the Punt across to Stockton. We would spend the entire day. Auntie Gert would always make Scones and Pumpkin/Gramma pie especially for my father! Norm and Gert were my Nana Millies brother and sister.

One other place we went was at Mardi, Uncle Hilt and his wife Annie. Hilt was my Nana Millies Uncle, my Great, Great uncle. Their property was amazing to me. Their house was old, older than any house I had ever been in. They had chooks, ducks, and geese running freely everywhere, I can still remember the smells and the noises! Uncle Hilt never wore shoes around the yards, the poop and mud would ooze up between his toes as he plodded around collecting eggs for us to take home. I loved it! As a family we attended their 50th Wedding Anniversary in 1962, too young to remember, but this old couple shared their celebrations with their siblings, you see, Auntie Annies two brothers Frederick and Thomas, married Uncle Hilts two sisters Lavinia and Evelyn the same day in 1912, triple Wedding! The last time I saw this old couple, Hilt and Annie were at their 60th Wedding Anniversary in 1972, there were only two couples left as Thomas and Evelyn had passed away!

My mother was a very controlling person! I remember as a youngster when we went visiting dad's uncle norm and aunty Glady, I would sit in a chair not game to move because of the warnings I had had before going there and the threat of a belting if I put a foot out of place, as she use to say. When offered a biscuit for afternoon tea I would look at mum to make sure it was all right to have one. Dad's aunt Glad always had Arnott's orange slice and chocolate creams, I would have been devastated if she didn't give a nod. That biscuit would last forever. I would twist it part, lick out the cream centre before finishing it off. I got this idea from Uncle Norm he always did it and would raise his eyebrows look at me doing the same and smile as he dipped his biscuit halves in his cup of tea.

Over the years to come I saw acts of violence no child should be subjected to or be witness to. There were days I never wanted to come home from school. I can't find the words to describe my feelings as I got off the school bus each afternoon! Not knowing what was or had already happened inside that house!

At school I could be someone else and my friends Kym, Julie, Michelle, Jan, and Wendy, were my sanity, but I could not talk to them about my home life. We talked about boys, clothes, etc and because we all had siblings my friends and I use to talk about our love hate relationship with them. For me back then I only had one sibling and mine, I thought, held me back from developing and adventuring my teenage life as my friends did. Siblings are individuals, but our mother, the way she brought us up, wanted us to be the same, almost twins!

We were always dressed in identical clothes and shoes, sometimes, different a colour, her in blue and me in pink, but the same. Our hair was always styled the same way and everything I did she had to do. I felt left behind, I was probably, the only 15/16year old who could not join her friends, Saturday afternoon at the pictures, after school at the local pool, netball on weekends, shave my legs or under my arm, pluck my eyebrows, where lip gloss or any kind of make-up, all a no, no! Cause mum said I had to wait till my sister could do it too! The only things I was in line for first was when we went to the Doctors to have our boosters, measles, mumps, whooping-cough and polio, I would always get my injections first, roll my sleeve up and it was all over so quickly, but, when it was my sisters turn, she would scream, cry, run around the surgery trying to get away, they would have to hold her down to give her the injection. I went to kindergarten and High School on my own. Oh! and I got my Periods and wore a bra first. What is wrong with being the oldest child in a family? I thought it was to lead the way for your siblings.

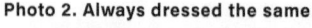
Photo 2. Always dressed the same

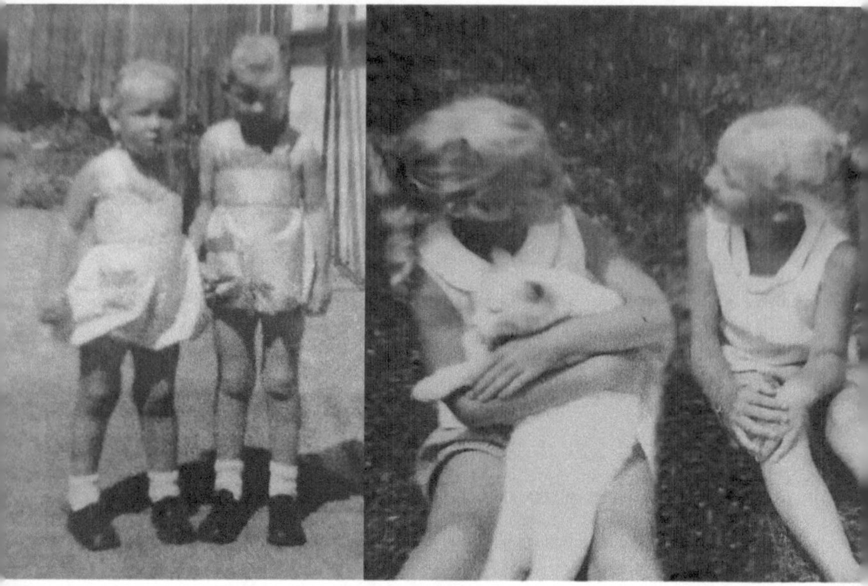

Because of the way things were at home my head was full of dread and fear, my schoolwork suffered, I had no self-confidence, I lost the ability to concentrate, and I absorbed nothing in class. The day would soon be 3pm and I would have to go home. I could not invite my friend's home; they might see or hear something that I could not bare them knowing.

Looking back, I believe some neighbours would have had to know something about what was going on inside our house. 461 Orange Grove Road was on the high side of a waterfront road. The sounds most have travelled. There was plenty of banging and that yelling, and occasionally it was me yelling at them to stop. Why didn't someone call the police? Why didn't anyone knock on our door? Why didn't my mother just leave? Why did she stay and subject herself and her offspring to the violence. Years later I was to have the answers to some of these questions.

Sometimes my father would come home in an obviously bad mood, but mum would not leave him alone, she would nag and aggravate him in front of us. Then when the fight really started Mum would yell at my father 'Hit me hit me'. 'You will feel better after you have hit me'. I wondered why she just did not leave him alone, eventually he would hit her. I still cannot believe they were so involved in making each other miserable that they did not see the horror on their daughters faces!

One day Dad walked through the door with a rifle by his side. I thought he was going to shoot my mother, but he actually, wanted my mother to shoot him. Then he turned the gun and wanted to shoot her. With the barrel pushed in her stomach he pushed her backwards to the bathroom and into the bathtub right over into one corner. I just stood there through the whole ordeal waiting for the bang. I do not remember a word spoken fright muffled their voices, but I saw the whole terrible thing. Then it was over, no shot was fired, thankfully! I witnesses no more that day but that night I would relive it all over again in my sleep, through the bad dreams. No calm happy thought in my sleep. I had tortured dreams, my nightmares were real, re-enactments of what I had seen. Always horror! But the next day I could go to school, and pretend it never happened, except on weekends I hated the weekends.

On many a dark and depressing day, through total despair, in my thoughts I would try to figure out how to kill myself or disappear. I imagined if I did something to myself, maybe, just maybe, my parents would be different, change their cruel ways. I just wanted to do something to get their attention! On days when I was not desperate, I use to daydream about being abducted by a spaceship and taken far, far, away!

Not making excuses for my parents, but children

born around the 1930's must have had a tough upbringing, but my father's childhood was terrible. He was born in Parramatta, his parents having to marry as Nana Millie was pregnant. He grew up in Carlingford in a home with no father around; his father, my Grandfather Sherlock, believed that the last-born child, a daughter was not his but the product of my Grandmother Millie's infidelity, with a male friend whose name was Joe. Sherlocks occupation was a truck driver, my dad was about 5yrs old when he left his wife the twin boys, newborn girl, and moved to Darwin. There he stayed sending no child support, money, till about 1962 when he moved back, to a suburb of Sydney either Smithfield or Fairfield.

Meanwhile back in Carlingford, my grandmother Millie put the children in the Delmar Homes and again in 1946 the younger 3 were sent to Carlingford Children's Home for 2 more years. She wrote on their enrolment form she was of ill health, but her occupation as a machinist allowed her to contribute 10/- a week for each child. Family rumours while the children were in the home say there was a lot of men coming and going from her home all hours. Or she had had a lot of boyfriends?

My father hated it in the children's home. he would run away back home every chance he got, sometimes taking his twin brothers with him, so I have been told. When he was old enough, possible about 12/13 he got a job on an ice and milk cart to help his mother with the bills. All my fathers' life he was a hard worker. He was also an incredibly generous person throughout his life. Starting with his twin brothers, he would send money to them, if they needed it (they both lived in far Queensland). When their mother Millie died in 1980, he paid for their travel down to the funeral and gave them a place to stay for as long as needed. He also gave his time to help people. Dad's best friend Bill, and his wife Valda, friends he had had since his childhood days at Carlingford, had a son Robert, who was brain-damaged after a motor bike accident. Dad went to their home most afternoons, on his way home, even if it was only for a few minutes. He helped with Robert's care and on the day that Bill had to tell Robert that my father was no longer coming around because he had died, Robert took an epileptic fit, never recovered, and was buried exactly 1 week after my dad, at the same place and is buried just a few graves away. Eventually, Valda and their other son Wayne were also buried there, and it was also Bills wish to be put with them all!

My mother was the third last child born in a family of twelve plus children. Her mother my Grandmother Maria (pronounced Mariah) had her first child in 1911 (father unknown) a daughter. She may have given this child to one of her sisters to raise, details are incomplete, her name was Rita. Maria married October 1912 William; they were together till William's death in 1970. Maria's 2nd child a son was stillborn Nov 1912, buried unnamed. Then from Oct 1913 to 1934 they had 12 children. Was there enough love in this home to go around all these children? Nana Maria who lived to be 102 years old never spoke of the 2 children born before 1913, they were only discovered by me accidentally.

I was off work for quite some time, recovering, after an accident at my workplace, breaking a bone in my lower back, the Sacrum. I could never return to this line of work, as bending, lifting, and on my feet all day was part of this job. Anyway, home for day after day, I got interested in my Family History, who were they, was there any criminals, what was their origin? Also remembering my father talk of his maternal grandmother Ruby, how wonderful she was to him & the fact she had died on his 12th birthday. It was through interest in this research, I discovered nana Maria's not talked about and unknown children's births. They have been placed with the family group!

My mother was a Hairdresser in the small country town where she was born. I grew up knowing all my mother's siblings as my father loved spending holidays with any of them, especially Jean and her husband Frank. My father was running a bakery in the main street, when I was born in 1954, 6 months after my parents married (I found this out when I was about 18). Fourteen months later my sister came along, and mum got rhematic fever. This was the second time in her life she had this. The first time was when she was about 6years old, but in 1955 she was in Hospital for a long time. I was sent to live with mum's older sister Jean who already had 4 children of her own. I suppose there was no other option as Dad had to run the bakery. I must have seen my father over these weeks as he remained a part of my new surroundings. However, my mother was a stranger to me, and I was told in later years I wanted nothing to do with her the day she arrived to take me home. This, apparently hurt her feelings. I was about 15 months old, have no memory of these days, but I would hear of how unhappy I made her feel later in my life.

Not too many years after that we relocated, to Carlingford. Living with dad's mother Millie for a while. My father worked these 3 jobs back then, a bakery at night, sawmill in the afternoon and a chicken farm at weekends. He eventually saved the money to buy his mother's house. What time did her have for himself; he was so busy providing for his family. Dad had no leisure time back then I was only about 6 years old, but I remember he was always walking out the back door with a lunch box.

Back then shopping days were once a fortnight in Parramatta. We travelled by bus; it picked us up on Pennant Hills Road near the K13 Submarine Memorial site. It was a long walk to the top of the hill, to catch that bus, on little, short legs. On the return home, we got off the bus with groceries, mum would divide the bags up, leaving either my sister or myself, mostly me, and half the grocery bags at the bus stop while walking home with what she could carry. On arrival home she left that one child and groceries in the empty house and walked all the way back to the one left minding the other bags. It had to be more than a mile one way. Scary, how did she not get one of us abducted! I remember being so hungry waiting for her to return, I picked a hole in the meat and ate some sausage mince! This was before starting school.

I went to Burnside Public School, near Parramatta, it was a bit of a long bus trip for a 5yr old, but Dad said I was not going to Carlingford Public. Maybe it was because of his memories there.

We moved when I was about 9years old to the house at 461 Orange Grove Rd.

461 the white fibro house was where I saw these mind crippling beatings and acts of violence. The house was elevated with brick footings across the front about four feet up from ground level at its highest point. This brickwork stretching right across the length of the house, continued around the corner and up the right-hand side about quarter the distance up the depth on the side closest to the neighbouring fence line. There was a strip of grass between the house and the fence just wide enough

for the lawn mower. On the other side of the house was the driveway and an open carport.

There were no steps to the front patio, the only door in and out of the house was around the back.

Behind that brick wall my mother had a good hiding spot, not to be seen from any angle. Mum had setup on the earth floor an old pan toilet seat with a black durable plastic or Bakelite lid, for a seat, a few supplies, including some paperback novels. I was searching for four leaf clovers around there when it all came into view. I walked in for a closer look. Where she had positioned everything, she could rest her back on the brick wall. Above her head were lots of webs and Daddy long leg spiders. I stood staring. With the timber flooring above, footsteps could be clearly heard. I knew why!

If the factory had called dad to come in through the night because someone had not turned up for their shift, or machinery had broken down, my father would get that phone call, we were used to the phone ringing through the night and hearing the car start. After that interrupted sleep dad came home for a rest, then go back to work, after. Obviously, she was avoiding him. They saved their confrontations for times when their children were around. I remember just looking around at this dark dingy space, all these questions I had, but no-one to ask!

Why did Mum just not leave? Dad tried to make her go, but she stayed… Later she said she stayed for us! Really! What could be worse! Then she said she had nowhere to go. Mum always reminded us that when they were dating, Dad played football, and during a game Dad was accidentally kicked in the head, had a Cerebral Haemorrhage and he changed, that is why he had violent turns toward her?

As each week went by sometimes, I would not come out of my room to see what was happening, the beatings continued, and my mother was a guilty as my father for my mixed-up emotions and fears. After their fighting she would intern fight with anyone around her and sometimes it was me. She was cruel both physically and verbally, never holding back and she was unpredictable. If I tried to stay out of her way, I was told I was up to something because quiet people could not be trusted. I was constantly told but for me, she would not be stuck with my father. I did not know what that meant at the time. I could not do anything right and it would never be any different for me.

One day I missed the bus home from Gosford pool. I was having swimming lessons, and I was slow getting dried and dressed. I caught the only bus that was outside the pool unfortunately it turned off at the bottom of mountain and I had to walk the rest of the distance home, but it didn't bother me.

As I got halfway up the street, I could see my mother walking toward me. She was wearing her apron, she always wore one of those, her hands behind her back, and in her hand was the wooden spoon. She tried to hit me with it, but I avoided her and ran all the way home closely followed by her still swiping at me. I dived under my bed to avoid the spoon. As she tried to hit me, she hit the wrought iron bed support and the spoon snapped in half. She was left holding the handle. Mum only had the one wooden spoon, so I avoided the welts that day. You never got a chance to explain, you were guilty no matter what the reason. She didn't know how to listen or to rationalise there would be a reason for being late.

Imagine what happen to me when my mother thought I was a thief. It was a Friday afternoon I had borrowed a friend's Scissors at school and had not given them back. Unfortunately for me my friend told her mother I had those scissors. Her mother must have written the letter straight away asking for those scissors to be returned because after school the following Monday my mother was waiting for me with her punishment. I had returned those scissors at school that day, but this made no difference to my punishment as she had received a letter and found it embarrassing. My friend's mother had no idea what writing that letter put me through. They were unaware of my mother's way of handling things and what went on in our home. Because I told no one!

I just sort of half existed through this time. I bordered on the edge. I bit my nails till they bled I was a bundle of nerves as I became a constant witness to my parent's violence, it was hell. At night I would sleep with my head under the covers, I would pull my legs up into my chest and wrap my arms around them. If one part of my body would get out from those bed clothes I would wake-up and quickly get myself organised, hidden again so I could go back to sleep. Some episodes are just a blur, but others are truly clear.

I can honestly write that through all the violent outbursts by my mother and father, surprising as it may seem, my father never ever threatened or harmed me or my sister in any way. He never smacked us, so I was never afraid of my dad. I just never considered the mental abuse he had inflicting on us. Neither did he! The only memory I have of Dad lashing out at me was one night when I was drying the dishes with my sister. We were arguing over something, I called her a slut. It was a word I had heard that day at school and I suppose I felt it may be a good word to use, but my father came from nowhere grabbed me by the ponytail and the back of my P.Js. My feet rose from the ground to tippee-toes as he hustled me out the back door and slammed the door behind me, saying do not use that kind of language in this house, and don't come back inside till I calm down. I didn't know whether I was to calm down or my father was to do the calming, but I stood outside anyway for some time long enough that when I came back in all the dishes were wiped and put away. My sister had to do it all on her own, so I felt she had shared the punishment.

It was around this time I was getting unbelievably bad pains in the stomach, head aches I just feel ill all the time. I complained to my mother repeatedly for weeks, but she just kept telling me I would live. I did not know what was wrong with me. One night when I went to bed, I kept thinking I might die because the pains were so bad!

The next morning, I woke-up and the sheets were covered with blood. It was everywhere, what was going on! After a few seconds I got over the site of all the blood, I calmed down and knew, this is what some of my girlfriends at school had had happen to them and now it was my turn. I went in to tell my mother, she opened her wardrobe door, and she had a bag of her old used elastic sanitary belts. Well, she pulled out one; it was all discoloured and rolled up on itself. As I held it in my hand, she gave me two pads and said to me, 'clean yourself up put one on now and take the other one to school you will need to change through the day.' I was so unhappy. She must have known why I had been in pain for weeks and she never even had a thought to have a new or clean sanitary belt put aside for me. I also needed more than one spare pad at school; luckily, the office lady at school had a caring nature and a cupboard of supplies for girl's needs. She also told me to get myself a little plastic zip purse to carry my pads in. Another shock was to know that this was going to be an ongoing thing. As if life was not bad enough now each month, I was going to experience cramping pain and bleeding. My mother told me nothing!

As time went on Dad did all different kinds of things that I thought strange. Once he took all mums clothes out of the wardrobe and she only had the clothes she wore that day. Then he bought them back, but not all of them. Some were never seen again. I thought taking her clothes odd as I thought mum didn't leave the house much. But I really didn't know!

Even through these terrible years, each Christmas, Dad always took us down south to where I was born to stay with my mother's family for a few days. These holidays I always saw my father enjoy himself. He really loved being there and enjoyed their company. It was as if, for a time, we were all different people, and it was exciting and happy times for all. But I didn't understand, if mum was so close to her family why didn't she get help from one of her sisters or brothers. What was her reason? Shortly after we got home things went backwards again. My parents would get back to the same old miserable existence. Hate and violence ruled their lives.

Amongst my most vivid memories of how one of these trips south began wasn't at Christmas time, it was the weekend of my 14th birthday. One of mum's nieces was getting married and we were on our way for a wedding. I was excited driving there I knew things would be good for a while. We started the trip and planned to stop at Parramatta to buy either, a wedding gift, or clothes to wear, to the wedding, I can't remember which, but after shopping we were well on our way. I had a battery-operated record player and some 45's, not many but and I listened (and my family) to the same music over and over again. Anyway, when I was changing a record Dad said, put the music up for a while and look under my seat I have a present there for you.' I unwrapped the present there was a necklace with matching earrings, blue and white beads on it. I thought it was beautiful. But I soon would hate it. As I put it on my parents started to argue, then pushing, hitting, and shoving, all this while driving down the highway. I knew straight away it was over my birthday present,

I remember feeling guilty and that awful sick feeling came over me. As I tried not to think about it, I searched the road ahead for that big tree I looked forward to seeing on each trip it had a sign under it, "While I Live I Grow", as I gazed out the front window of that small white V.W. we went everywhere in, the next thing I knew mum's side door flew open and she tried to jump out. My father grabbed her arm and held her inside the car while he turned off into the dirt on the side of the road. They continued to argue and fight, then Dad got out of the car and started to walk back into the direction we had come. He was headed home on foot. The traffic streamed passed us and the big trucks made our little car rock. It was bad enough being trapped in the back of that V.W. while they fought, no bedroom to go off to, no T.V. to lose myself in, there was no hiding from what just happened and now the only person who could drive the car was walking home. I started to panic, didn't anybody here know he was walking away, fast. My mother, my sister weren't saying anything, so I started to yell then scream out the window, come back. My mother told me to shut-up, then she said if you want him to come back so bad go after him and stop that screaming. So, on the edge of that busy Hume Hwy on the beginning of a long weekend holiday break I got out of the car and ran as fast as I could to catch up. At first, he didn't hear my yelling, but when he did, he turned, and I beckoned him back. After a short hesitation he did walk back, I didn't wait, but when I got back in the car my eyes were fixed out the rear window to make sure he was still walking in our direction. Soon as he got back behind the wheel, he turned the car around and headed back for home. That night I lay all knotted up in my bed, head under the sheets, not sleeping at all. The next morning to my surprise we set off again and made it to the wedding. I left the necklace and earrings at home.

Months went by things stayed the same. Then my grandmother, Millie moved from Queensland with her boyfriend. I really didn't remember her from the days we lived with her in Carlingford, but she used to send presents through the post when we were younger. Mainly clothes she had made for us. She also gave me her old sewing machine the only time I remember her visiting us in 461 Orange Grove Rd, a few years before. I loved to sew, I was learning at school, and someone must have told her. I would have been about 11 years old then because I used that sewing machine to make my first dress to wear to a school dance the last year in primary school. I was really looking forward to getting to know that nana. She made all her own clothes dad had told me and she had made my Christening robe. (I have kept it in good condition for my children and hopefully their children to wear).

The house at Carlingford was rented out for a while, but dad eventually sold it to purchase an Orchard, 25 acres. There was an older style house there, but, my mother did not want to live there, I was a long drive. Dad bought chooks, turkeys, geese, and pigs for his farm. He would go there every day after work, to feed and look after his animals.

I don't remember exactly when this all came about, but Nana Millie and her boyfriend moved onto dad's farm. We just went there one day, and they were living in the house, of course with dad's permission. Dad seemed all wrapped up in this farm and after school we would wait out the front of the house, 461 Orange Grove, dad would pick us up and drove the 40 minutes out to the farm to feed the animals, and we saw and did get to know our nana,

Millie. Mum didn't join us much on weekdays, but she came weekends.

Days and weeks rolled on, then one day, things got out of control again. It began with the usual yelling and pushing each other around then dad went into a rage grabbing my mother by the throat trying to shut her up. He pushed her across the small hallway and up against the linen press. As I came into full view, I could see her feet were off the floor. My mother's face was red; Dad was really shutting her up this time. I was going to have to do something. This was not the time to run and hide, so I started to yell for Dad to let her go, you are choking her I yelled. I knew I had to do something more. As I searched the room for something to throw at Dad. Beside me was the cupboard where mum kept the brooms and odds and ends that would usually be stored in a garage, but we only had a car port at our house. The first thing my eyes caught sight of was a wooden handle, so I grabbed it. It was heavy but I pulled it out quickly then I saw it was a small axe. There was no time to think, I had to get my father's attention somehow, so I raised it above my head and yelled at my father 'look at me I'm going to hit you with this if you don't let her go'. He spun around; our eyes were glaring at each other. After a few seconds he loosened his grip and Mum slid to the floor. Dad looked at me with his deep blue eyes, for the first time I was afraid of my father, and he knew it. He walked straight past me and out the back door. Mum got up off the floor and never said a word. She never even said thank you. The next few hours I spent in my room (which I shared with my sister) listening to my music, Dad must have come home for dinner that night, but I don't remember. Mealtimes were always the same. We waited for dad to get home before we ate, why I don't know, mealtimes were less than enjoyable, every piece of food must have stuck in my neck. Who wanted to waste time chewing, shovel it in and get away from the table as quickly as possible, get away from the hateful glares, snappy voices, and miserable faces, that night would have been like every other. I would have put my head down, ate and probable didn't look at either of them.

To my room again I went as quickly as possible after drying the dishes. I could not sleep so I lay awake, I could hear someone crying very softly, I crept to the bedroom door and stood quietly listening, then I realised it was my father. I crept across the hall to see if I could see more clearly, I knew he saw me, so I said, 'are you alright'. He didn't answer me, so I turned to go back to bed, then Dad said, 'come here for a moment'. I was not afraid as I was that afternoon and I walked straight in without hesitating. There was a streetlight right out the front of the house so I could see my father lying in bed. As I stood alongside the bed, he grabbed my hand and said he was sorry for everything. He told me he could not control his anger at my mother. Dad asked me to forgive him; he said all he wanted was to hear me say, that I could forgive him. He also said that I would never see him hit my mother again. So, I forgave him, and I meant it! That was that and I felt good he had thought to ask for forgiveness but as I walked back to my room my mother who had been knitting in the lounge room saw me. She asked what you are doing in there and I said I could hear Dad crying and I told her the words that Dad and I had exchanged. Mum was furious; she said I had no right to forgive him it was not my place to do such a thing! and get back to bed! I felt I had done the right thing I told my father what he wanted to hear, and he kept his word

I never saw him attack Mum physically again. I saw the occasional black eye, fat lip or bruise but I never saw him do it. As for Mum, she would never let me forget that I had no right to forgive him for anything. My mother had difficult looking at me after that. She did not know how to forgive or forget anything. (I realised this as an adult.)

Crying nonstop, nervous, emotional, the anxiety of what to expect next, and nothing to look forward too. The thoughts of suicide were the worst, but I could not get it together.

I don't remember when this exactly was, packing my bag and on a train to go down south to stay with mum's mother Maria. Alone, I had to change trains at Central to a really long train and again at Cooma to another train that looked more like a bus, one carriage on a one lane railway line, it took hours to get there, I am still amazed to this day that I was allowed to travel so far alone. I was there on my own for the first time ever. I had total freedom. Unfortunately, my poor Nana Maria didn't know what to do with me, I was a bored teenage girl with emotional problems, who didn't know what to do with herself in a country town and when I wasn't walking up and down the small main street I just sat around. While I was there one of mum's sisters Aunty Mavis who lived in Canberra visited, so Nana sent me on with her, she had 5 children of her own, so I fitted in there and had a wonderful time. I was sent back on another train, changing at Central again, which got me home after mid-night. Dad picked me up from the station, he was furious, but not at me, at the hours I was alone on a train, as he carried my bag up the station steps, he rambled on about the time and didn't people have more sense!

As time went on none of us had any real relationships with each other no-one really talked or shared their feeling or the day's activities, no-one knew anything about anybody living in 461 Orange Grove Rd.

I walked in the door of that house each afternoon and could not wait to walk back out. I was now 15 years old.

One day after school my sister and I were having an argument. We never had much in common, growing up mum use to play us off against each other and watch what happened, we got use to not talk to each other about much, but we would argue, let's face it we had good teachers. Well right in the middle of it all, mum, who had been listening to it all from the kitchen came rushing in yelling how she needed peace and quiet how sick she was of listening to us bicker and how she was going to have a baby. I just stared at her. She was wearing one of those aprons she lived in, and she did look a bit fat, but pregnant. No way! How did that happen? Mum was nearly 40 years old, and about 5 or 6 months along. As I stared at her I realised I had not seen any bruises on her and things were a bit different. I figured Dad must know!

I can only remember a handful of visitors who stayed overnight with us in Orange Grove Rd. The first were My mothers 2 brothers who were not married. Uncle Keith a lovely quiet man who would later marry in 1972, but have no children, the other was Uncle Bill, who would never marry. Uncle Bill was a torment and a tease to all his nieces and nephews, he would pull ears or squeeze your cheeks. But worst of all if he saw any of us enjoying a lollipop, he would snatch it and throw it away.

Anyway, my sister and I had to give up our room to them and sleep on the old yellow vinyl night and day (as they use to be called) in the lounge room. After they left, I was sent into, strip the bed, change the sheets as instructed by my mother. On my bedside table I had a small fish tank and one little Goldfish. My fish was gone! I was frantic searching under the bed, behind the cupboard. No sign of my fish! I was sure Uncle Bill had something to do with his disappearance.

My parents made a phone call a few days later, but neither of mum's brothers knew what happened to my fish!

So that was that!

A few weeks went by and one night after bedtime, 8.30. (Remember when you made a long-distance call, you waited till after 8.30 to get a cheaper rate), so when the phone rang, you knew it was long distance! Dad answered it, I could hear him laughing, for ages. Next, Dad asked if I was still awake and came into the room, still laughing. He said Uncle Bill has found your fish….! He was getting dressed and pulled out a pair of shoes he had not worn since their visit, and there was my fish, all dried-up in the toe of his shoe. Poor fish must have jumped out of the tank and that is where he landed! Dad was still laughing! I told you Uncle Bill had something to do with his disappearance!!

The second couple to visit and stay the night, was while mum was pregnant a cousin from down south got married and we didn't go to the wedding. This was the first time my parents missed a family gathering, that Bride Janice could not believe it either, so they popped in on their honeymoon. Well, I don't know who got the biggest shock my cousin or Mum, who was more than obviously pregnant now and had to admit it. I am grateful to my cousin Janice because if she hadn't seen mum expecting, I think the family may have thought the new baby was mine or my sisters. I bet mum never considered this when she was trying to hide her pregnancy.

In early 1970 I had a beautiful baby brother, perfect in every way and I could not wait to see him. Scot was his name, and he was like a breath of fresh air in that house.

Life changed so much. During each school holidays for the next year Dad gave me a job in the shop and office at the front of the factory he managed, I had pocket money and a different kind of freedom, dressing-up, going some-where different from 9 to 3, seeing my father in his workplace and meeting new people.

At home now it was also different. With our main focuses on the baby, it was a quieter place but what had happened in that house over those past few years had fixed an uneasy atmosphere, so I always had that nervous sick feeling when I walked through that back door. It was my last year at school and in the half yearly exams I came top in my class.

Photo 3. School time

Having done so poorly at school I felt I had come along way battling my depressed feelings, emotions, and nervousness. I received a book prise for achievement and on presentation day parents were invited. But I received my book prise without my parents watching on. They were among those parents who did not turn up. I was on my own. I accepted that book as if it was worth millions.

Mum got her driver's licence and started driving us to school. In the last few weeks of the school term that year, as I hurried out of the car on the morning of my final Exam, it was Geography, for my School Certificate, I jammed my finger in the car door squashing my finger and popping my fingernail out of the already nibbled off area around it. The pain! I wrapped it in my hankie got back in the car next to my baby brother and Mum drove me to the chemist shop to buy a bandage. I showed my wrapped finger to the chemist for him to look at. As he opened my hankie, I saw the damage and fainted. Smelling salts brought me around, they sat me in a chair. I was in so much pain I heard the chemist say she needs to see a doctor, but I had a baby brother and my mother had to take him home for his sleep. So, in her wisdom, she bought some pain killers, took me home to bed. I don't know if mum rang the school to tell them what had happened, I slept all day and night, I slept through the pain!

I was not given my School Certificate because I didn't have a doctor's certificate to prove I wasn't in a fit condition to sit for my exam. I cried and cried! My future was ruined! Dad was furious that this had happened because this meant, we thought, I wouldn't get into Tech, but I did, and Dad helped organised it. I finished a year at Tech. After Tech I went to work permanently for the same company my father managed but a different depot.

Through that last year of school and the year at Tech I remained quiet and only mixed with a small group of friends, I joined a Fellowship and spent a lot of time at friends' houses, where there parents seemed to have had happy relationships, I saw things in them that was missing in my parents and I was draw like a magnet to their homes, lucky for me I always felt welcomed. But now my friends and I had our jobs we were all busy working.

We adjusted to life not seeing each other every day as we had done for years. We had boyfriends and our lives had changed no longer schoolgirls, but young adults. Though years have passed we are all still in touch. Now my friends and I use the phone to stay connected, but with an 'hello' it is as if we were together yesterday, but, I have never shared the detail of what went on in 461 Orange Grove.

All that filled my mind as a young woman was to get married and leaving home. Those thoughts filled my dreams, and I became engaged at 18 to the first real boyfriend I had. I never had an engagement party or any fuss I didn't care about that I was simply happy, I had someone to talk to and confide in and I could spend as much time as I liked at his parents' home and less and less time with my family.

One day on my arriving home my mother was in her usual cranky mood by now I had learnt to switch off entirely, it must have been some kind of self-preservation to stay normal for now, I looked forward to the time with my baby brother. Anyway, this day she barked at me, 'if you are sleeping with that boy, you had better marry him as no-one else will ever want you'! I did not even look at her when she said this, I just didn't understand what she was on about!

Well, my life was busy, filled with work, saving and romantic plans. The wedding was booked for March. My father was unhappy to say the least; he could not stand my fiancé I could probably go so far as say he hated him, and Dad knew I was making a big mistake. Dad never told me why he didn't want me to marry him, but I wouldn't have listened to his reasons or cared at that time because I never stopped to consider anything past marriage, renting a house and moving out and onto happily ever after! I went along with everything decided for me about the wedding. My little brother was Pageboy, and I had to have my sister as a Bridesmaid, even though we had nothing in common and I would have preferred one of my girlfriends whose parents' houses I spent so much time, but I agreed with everything. It kept the peace and as this would be, I thought, the last time I would ever have to do as I was told. I continued dreaming of the future and what I thought it would be.

Only months before my wedding several things happened that should have fazed me or at least snapped me into reality but none of these events did. First my Fiancé' asked me to lend him the money to buy my engagement ring. He said his father had seen one in the city and he wanted to get it for me, I can't remember how much I handed over, but I paid for my own ring. Then his car was stolen. I was so devastated for him. In the midst of all this I was in my room at home where I spent most of my time when home; out in the lounge room I could hear the crying and loud voices of my family. I clearly heard my Mum was saying "how can you do this to me?" Do what, I listened more closely but my brother was in bed asleep, so they were trying not to yell. But I could make out my sisters' boyfriends voice too, then Dad's voice. It was all confusing. Nothing had been said for a while when my sister walked into the room. She said get yourself another bridesmaid, I do not want to be your Bridesmaid, A comment like that didn't surprise me, we didn't get along rarely talked and went off in different direction, but I asked the question anyway, Why? 'Because I'm Pregnant she squealed'! Well, this was unexpected, but then again, she too had been spending as much time as she could away from our house and at her boyfriends. I asked her why she wasn't on the Pill if she was having sex. 'Are you' she asked, I said yes. Then she accused me of letting her down by not telling her so she could have avoided this, but I explained I had the guidance of a girlfriend's mother about 6 months before, and as she was 14months younger than me, so why would I consider she needed that kind of advice. But it made no sense to her. Dad never said much about the whole mess. He was actually very calm and supportive towards my sister and her situation, but she too had grown so distant from him. She had less of a relationship than I. I do not think she ever noticed his heart felt concerns. Even though Mum herself had to marry being pregnant with me she did not have any kind words of support! Anyway, I cannot write anymore, the rest is my sisters' story to tell! I stayed out of the way through this time, and I didn't ask any questions. I didn't express my feelings, especially around my mother for if she did not like your opinion or openness she would give you a smack around the ears, so why bother, it was safer to hide your emotions and concerns and stay out of it.

At this point I was counting down the days to the Wedding. I never took into consideration I was marrying for life. Was I really in love, what was that anyway? It was not what I saw at home. The invitations went out the church and the reception were booked, then I found out my fiancé's car was not stolen it was repossessed. He had no money. He had a gambling problem, and to top it all off, I took my engagement ring into the jewellers to have it cleaned so it would be as shinny as my wedding band. When I went to pick it up, the shop assistant, who I knew from school said, I must tell you this, it is not a diamond or precious stone in this ring. I felt my heart sink! How else was my future husband going to disappoint me? Where did the money go that I gave him for the ring? You know, I didn't care! They were only material thing. I just kept thinking it would get better; it had too, how could things get worse. I couldn't imagine. I was so naive!

The wedding day: the white dress, my sister was the bridesmaid, Mum saw to that! Walking up the isle Dad said in a faint voice; it would be worth all the embarrassment and don't even consider the money spent, just turn around with me and go back out the door. I just ignored my father even spoke to me and I just kept walking towards the Alter. I wanted a new life, and I thought that person at the other end of that aisle, with all his faults, was the one who could make a happy life for me. that "Happily Ever After" was the way it was meant to be and it began with marriage, I thought.

"No" I was wrong, and Dad was right. After just a few months of marriage suddenly I woke-up, all my plans and dreams had been nothing more than a lot of happy endings from old movies that I had put together in my head and the reality of my life was a big disappointment to me. I was not in control of my life, and I had to do something about it. I could feel an emotion coming over me and I didn't want it to take hold. I knew I had to get a grip on things. My husband's gambling had not improved this caused arguments and tears. He thought to win he had to gamble bigger, and his habit got out of control. Things happened that became, to me, larger than life because of embarrassment and my disappointment in him! Once I went shopping for food and when I got to the check-out the money to pay for groceries was gone, just taken without a word and he let me walk down the street knowing my purse was empty. I started to hide money to pay rent and buy food; this was not me I hated that I had to do this. Then he stole money from a company he was working for. He had been to Court, he got a good behaviour bond, but now he couldn't get a job, so to try and prove he could turn his life around he joined the Army, we realised somewhere about then that we could not really be in love, but for a time we must have needed each other. I thought I could help him change, meet his commitments, making payment when they were due, saving, but he just could not do it, no will power, he could not give up the gambling. He proved this while in the Services he continued to gamble. He must have known he couldn't reform as soon as he was accepted into the Army, because we let the rented house go, sold all the furniture and paid off as much debt as the money allowed us, he left for Basic training and because I had nowhere to live and no savings left, I asked my parent if I could move back into my old bedroom. Yes, I moved back to 461 Orange Grove Rd. I never tried to work at my Marriage we both knew it was over and we have never seen each other again, not even passed in the street. We each went our separate ways. I was now 21 years old.

After moving what little I had left, and I was back to the place I was so desperate to escape I did not know how I was going to cope. I had no plans I just took each day on as it came. But I was grateful for somewhere to live and for the privacy I got as no-one ever discussed my short marriage or asked why about anything, you see I think, no-one really cared as the distance that had been put between us would never change. We all just stayed out of each other's way. Mum was still the same and she could still push Dad's button. They fought, argued, snapped, and sneered at each other that hadn't changed. I tried to make myself small, so it was not noticeable that I was there, mum still looked at me, on occasion, as she did the night, I forgave my father, and I didn't like eye contact with her. My sister was still living there, we still had nothing to talk about, and I knew she must have had as I did her own mental and emotional scars from watching on as our parents tortured each other with verbal and physical abuse, but we never discussed it. I did my own washing, helped in the kitchen, and tried not to get in anyone's way. I had left my job when things got embarrassing and I realised my marriage was over. It was too hard emotionally working for the same company as dad and I thought leaving was best at the time. I looked for another job. As the weeks went by all of us just tolerated each other I guess, sometimes my despair was so over-whelming

I just bordered on that edge again. I know we would be described as a dysfunctional family. Words fail me now, I cannot, describe what those few years since that Saturday afternoon had done. We were all just there. No feelings no emotions. Just breathing air, in, out, in, out. But through each breath our hearts were filled with love and hope, for the smallest member of this family, Scot. We all took interest in him as he went about his daily routines. His little antics amused us all. He was so lucky he had a life ahead of him with no visions of violence flashing through his head. I was so glad for him. I hoped good things for him, stability and direction, but most of all I hoped that our parents could think of him first as he gets older and when he is taking in their facial expressions, as they argue I hoped it would not affect him and don't let him witness any physical violence, so he doesn't become mixed-up as I thought I was.

1975 it was this year I met my soulmate, best friend, and husband. We married 1978 and I know love is a real feeling. It consists of the need to support, protect, listen with an open mind and heart, simply be there without condemnation. He had also been married before, no children but we have 3 children together. We are, I am pleased to say, a normal happy close family. To achieve normality, I had to make the decision to concentrate totally on Husband and children. This meant I could not keep going back trying to make sense of my childhood and the things I had seen. There were times I thought how wonderful things were, my new husband and my father got along so well and because of that I saw a lot of my dad.

Photo 4. Our 3 babies

When I gave birth to my 3 babies between Dec 1978 and Aug 1982 my parents showed interest in them and visited for cuddles but what surprised me the most was when my second baby was born, a son, my father came to the hospital to visit. Dad picked my son up out of the hospital cot and held him while chatting to me about how he was driving passed and thought he would just drop in. I felt so privileged he had done that. He put a happy feeling in my heart that day I will never forget it. Mum was kind enough to mind my 23-month-old daughter while I was in hospital for those 3 days. But when we went to pick her up mum said, "It is a shame you were not in hospital longer so this child could forget you and make you feel as you had made me feel when I had your sister and was so sick for all those weeks. I looked into her eyes; she was serious. She had held this grudge against me for about 25 years. I had no memory of this, and she was telling me now. I guarded my emotions and simply ignored she even spoke.

While raising my children I didn't rely on my mother for babysitting, she was always at tennis, squash or out with friends! There were times I thought a mother's help would be good, then there were incidents or accidents where I was around that made me want to do it myself. One day while at the farm my 2-year-old son was running to see the pigs & his grandfather who was feeding up, he fell into the runoff of sewerage, my husband quickly grabbed him by the back of his overalls and jumper dragging him out. The little fellow was covered in pig manure. We rushed him over to the house, to wash him down, my mother said, you are not bringing him into my bathroom, hose him off outside! It was winter or chilly weather, but we hosed his clothes, with him still in them, stripped him off, all the time him screaming from the cold! Then we were allowed to go into the bathroom, for that hot shower. Its days like these that are stuck in my head! So cruel! Me allowing it to happen because I was too afraid to insist on warm water, because I did not want to argue.

When there was a birthday or at Christmas time we would always join in with my dysfunctional family, I thought all 4 grandparents were important in my children's lives, but on my side we all had this problem relating to each other. The pasts had taken its' toll on us. The slightest little thing said would start the ball rolling and there would be hostility, anger, bad tempers, and yelling. The feelings developed years ago would surface then things that had happened in the past that should have been forgotten and more importantly forgiven, would be mentioned and blame was thrown around, fingers would be pointed. Sometimes at me! Then one day during one of these episodes I looked at my Husband and children's faces. I saw a look in their eyes I did not want to see. So, I said to myself that is enough family gatherings. I could take no risks with my children. My head screamed at me to get away they have seen enough. I had continued to fit my dysfunctional family into our lives and had suffered the consequences time and time again; my husband had to put up with my tears and depressed state. It was not fair to him. He had not lived in 461 Orange Grove Rd so he could never understand why I thought if I had to deal with them regularly, I would fail as a wife and mother. I had to distance myself.

I doubted myself and worried some days raising my children. I thought to myself, am I stable enough for this job. Was what my parents were, in my DNA? Was over the years to come a monster going to emerge or was I going to be the product of the environment

I grew up in? All this ran through my head as I was raising my babies! I had had no instruction and these little people depended on me. I had 3 children at home all day the youngest at this time was 6months old. Many mums would admit how tiring young children are. It's not just the physical tiredness it's the emotional tiredness as well, looking after their safety and wellbeing. Feeling overwhelmed one day I smacked one of them hard and several times, I felt guilty and wanted to take it back. I decided to tell our doctor. Talking to him he suggested some counselling and a discussion group for mums who were feeling inadequate. This counselling ran for several weeks, and I was glad to be able to talk to someone who didn't know me personally. Someone who may have had some answers to my fears and doubts. I opened up, about my childhood memories and my struggles to make sense of the past and how I didn't want it to influence my husband and small children through my everyday actions. I came away each day, a little more confident learning about moving on, and letting go of things that cannot be fixed. I came away reassured I was not my parents, and I was, capable of raising my children in a loving environment, but most importantly to me my parenting was not controlled by my parents.

I didn't see my extended family all together for a while. Mum and Scot would call in to see the kids from time to time. As we lived on the Pacific Hwy, Dad passed by often while working. Really early some mornings I would be woken from the sound of his footsteps coming up the concrete drive. He would leave a loaf of fresh bread on top of the metre box. I would say to my husband 'fresh bread for your lunch today' and we would smile at Dad's thoughtfulness. Sometimes when he saw me, he would give me a few dollars and tell me to go buy myself something. I know he would have done the same for my siblings. He was like that generous and fair. He also knew I had a good husband and didn't really need money but, it must have made him feel good!

Another time he stopped by about lunch time. I had just sat the kids at the table. I asked him did he want anything, but he said he was simply happy sitting on the lounge watching them. This day Dad was full of plans he said he was thinking of purchasing some land and building some kind of storage units to rent out as he was looking forward and planning a use for his long service money and his retirement. He said he had a doctor's appointment for a check-up as he had not had one for a while. I was busy feeding the baby and I did not even ask if he felt all right or if he was feeling ill. He also chatted about his dogs. Dad had Greyhound dogs. It was a hobby he loved and would travel to the track on weekends for races. Once he had a win and he went to an action to buy us carpet for our house. Until he arrived with it on the trailer, we had no idea he was thinking of doing this for us. We were renovating at the time and had ripped up the old lino floor coverings. Dad thought carpet for the little ones would be a good idea. We had it lying in the hall still rolled up for months waiting to finish painting etc. Dad never lived to see it laid.

Dad, mum, and Scot moved to the farm in mid 1978. My husband and I had also lived there for a time and were married under the big trees, in the garden. All this came about because the farmhouse had been unoccupied for some time. There had been a disagreement over a cousin who nana Millie (dad's mother) had brought down from Queensland, this all happened when I was in my last year of school. She was one of dad's twin brother's daughters. Both the twins were married to women who may have been of Aboriginal descendants and there were about 10 cousins I had never met. But because Beverley came to live with nana, I got to know her. She was only 5 months younger than me and had already left school. I was the first-born grandchild, and she came next. Beverley had a quiet nature; she was thin, taller than me and had dark hair. Her speech was noticeable different. At the end of every sentence, she had a habit of saying "A". Anyway, I liked her, and nana treated her a bit like a maid. Nana would say she is here to help out, she is not on a holiday. It became clear Beverly became unhappy living with nana and her man-friend. Dad and nana had a disagreement about Beverly's unhappiness after she had told my father how she had wanted to go home, and nana would not let her leave. Beverley must have told the farmer down the road where she used to go and help with the fruit picking and unbeknown to anybody, they had a plan. One night that farmer, and his wife, helped Beverley out her bedroom window and took her to the railway station; she caught a train back to her family in Queensland. They told Nana what they had done before they returned to their home. There was a huge argument. Nana, after this happened moved off the farm, she stripped the house, even taking things that were in the house when she moved in. I know dad would have eventually helped Beverley himself, but he probably didn't know how to go about it, if it meant interfering and it resulting in him fighting with his mother. Beverley's father did call dad at work to let him know she had arrived safely home. In 1992 I met up with Beverley when my husband took us on a holiday to Queensland. She was still a quiet person, married with small children. When talking about her experiences while living with our nana she told me she had never actually told my father how Nana use to treat her, she said she had not wanted to cause any trouble between dad and nana so that is why she had done what she did and involved the farmer and his wife up the road. It was good to finally hear all this.

Nana Millie died in 1980 she had left her man-friend and was living with her only daughter.

Mum and dad had planned to move to the farm, but before they did, dad wanted some renovations done to the old house. As my future husband was a builder, he had come to some agreement with my dad, as I said they got on well, and we moved in. While we lived in the old farmhouse rent free, we did the renovation and dad paid for the materials. It was good living on the farm, very peaceful. I got a new job and was happy. I would ride my 175 Yamaha trials bike down the hill to work. I didn't have a car licence and this little motor bike gave me independence. I did learn to drive on the old tractor while we were living there though, and this helped me in getting my car licence. Dad would still be there each afternoon to feed the animals. He had got interested in breeding pig as well as his greyhounds, so he would rush around feeding all these animals clean up, then head off home for dinner. Scot would be with him. On weekends dad and Scot were there all the time and dad's Uncle Norm, dad's mother's brother, towed his caravan up one weekend and decided to leave it there on the farm and he and his wife would arrive a couple of weekends a month and stay. There was always somebody around and I think dad, really liked all the company and to share what he had.

After my parents moved onto the farm it was too far for my father to go home through the day for his breaks from work, so he bought a house from some people he knew just a few doors from the factory he was still managing. It was about this time my father's father Sherlock started to visit my dad at his work and would drive up from Sydney. I had not really gotten to know him. I did not even know he was still alive. I never recall him ever visiting us at Orange Grove Rd, but there he was, and he asked my father if he could move into the house near the factory, and my father let him live there. I puzzled over this! I knew when my dad was about 21, he travelled to Darwin with his friend Bill, to meet up with his father whom he had not seen since he was young, but I had no idea if they had stayed connected or what was going on. My father had permitted his mother to move onto the farm, now his father turns up and he gives him a place to live.

1983 it was a Saturday. My friend from school, Kym, invited us over for Lunch. She had 2 small boys similar in ages to our kids. Kym had been living in Victoria since she left school, a year earlier than me. We had always remained friends and kept in contact. She only lived a 40minute drive away now so that day our husbands got to know each other, and our children played together. We didn't arrive home late, but

I bathed the kids, put them into their P.Js. gave them an early diner hoping to get them to bed early. I had just put the baby to bed with her bottle she was now 10 months old. Then the phone call came. A nurse introduced herself and said my father had suffered a heart attack and had not survived. He had been attending a reunion at Carlingford Public School, with classmates. Mum hadn't told Scot yet and she said that we had to be there with her at a school friend's of dad's home in Carlingford first thing the next morning so when my brother arrived back from where he was sleeping the night we would be there for him when he first heard the news of dad's death as he was so young. She also said I had to go over to my sisters to tell her our father was dead. I was in no state to drive a car, and my husband couldn't drive me as our babies were all in bed asleep, so I phoned her instead, it was the quickest and easiest way. After that I then had to call baby-sitters to come early Sunday morning. I had a wonderful friend who lived next door she had 5 daughters and she organised 2 of her girls to help me. I did not sleep all night waiting for daylight I could not believe my father was dead he was only 52.

Watching on as my brother was told was so painful. I wondered what would become of him no father at such a young age. He and mum sat in the back of our car on the way home, my sister and her husband drove dad's car. No-one spoke much but I know I kept asking my brother are you all right as he was too quiet.

Then there was the funeral. Mum said no children at the funeral I had to help with cups of tea and food. I wanted to do the right thing and I wanted to help. I couldn't get anyone to mind the three little ones, together, so I had to split them up and rely on friends to mind them for the entire day as my usual baby-sitters who minded them at our home, the girls next door, were in high school. We went early to view dads' body. Auntie Jean and Uncle Frank (they were who I lived with when my sister was born, and mum had rhematic fever) came with us. They drove from Canberra the day after they got the news dad had died and they were there to support mum and the rest of us. After seeing my father lying in his coffin, I can honestly say I don't remember much about my own father's funeral. I remember there were a hundred people there, but all their faces are just a blur. My

Nana, Maria mum's mum was there I saw her back at the farmhouse where the people were gathering after the funeral service. She had travelled with 2 of her sons. She was about 92 years old, but she said she was not going to let any of her family talk her out of travelling to attend this funeral. Nana lived to be 102 years old and all but the last year of her life after she fell and broke her hip getting firewood, she lived in her own home, so I suppose she knew she was up to the long trip. Later in the afternoon after most of the visitors were gone, I called one of my friends who was minding my 10-month-old, and I could hear my baby crying in the background I had had enough so we went home and collected all 3 kids on the way.

Quite a few days went by we all had to adjust. Auntie Jean and Uncle Frank went back home and one afternoon after my husband got home from work, we went up to the farm to help feed the animals. Mum was in a rotten mood. She had found out that I had not done as I was asked and gone to my sister in person to tell her of our father's death, that I had told her over the phone. I could not believe it. My husband said it was useless trying to talk to her and explain why, she should have realised for herself you were not capable of driving, so you used the phone. I coped the verbal abuse as usual!

Exactly one week had passed and we attended Robert's funeral. His parents were such good friends of dad's and dad spent all that time in their home helping with Robert's care. I had known this family all my life we spent a lot of time visiting and Robert use to lend me his motor bike to ride around their farm. We had to be there!

The next time I went to visit mum we were asked to be there. Mum had a bankbook for me, my sister, and my brother. Deposited in those 3 bank accounts was $5,000 each. I was amazed. I said thankyou and asked why she was giving us this money. She just said she could afford to. My brother had to leave his in the bank till he was 18, but it was a very generous I thought.

Over the next few months, then years, of course many things happened as life went on without dad. But a few details I remember clearly.

My mother had all dads' Greyhound dogs put down and buried. She said she didn't know what else to do there were so many of them. The pigs were sold. This took a while before they were all gone so they had to be fed daily and it was a big job, we helped. Foxes got most of the chooks and turkeys over time and there were only geese left.

Not long after that Mum took Scot on a holiday, it was a bus trip.

Life remained busy, our house renovations, small children, lending a hand at the farm if needed, my husband was particularly good about that, spreading himself thin. We also kept checking that Scot was ok. We had always been close, though there were 15 years between us and there was a time after I had my children he naturally felt left out as he had always been spoilt and the centre of attention, but basically, he was a good kid. We knew living with mum would not be easy and he would have been missing dad terribly as he had always followed him around the farm, or he was seen sitting in the front of dad's car or on the mudguards of the tractor while dad worked.

Scot and I use to chat. I always kept our line of communication open I didn't want him to ever feel he had no-one to talk too. During one of these chats, we talked about what we would do with the $5,000 mum had given us. He was going to buy a 4wheel drive and a motor bike, typical boy I though, as,

I chuckled to myself. Then he said something that set me back. Dad never got a chance to sign his new will you know. I said I didn't understand what he was talking about. There was a new will. Yes, he said but mum said it was an old one and dad made a new one this year. I was so upset, that meant Dad was worried about himself, his health, but he never said he felt that sick that he was compelled to update his will. I felt guilty I had not looked more closely at him or asked more questions when he said he had that Doctors appointment. I didn't ask Scot anymore question, he had moved on to the next thing he had on his mind.

Another day I took the kids out, don't remember where we were but Scot came. He was talking to this lady she had her arm around his shoulder giving him a big squeeze. After I asked him about that lady, he said she was the cleaner at school, I said how come you know her, I thought the cleaners came in after school was out, he said she does, but mum is late picking me up, so I help her. I said where's mum on those days, he said at tennis or squash. She did play those sports, well at least he had some company if he waited at school there was no-one at home.

Dad had been gone for some weeks now and one afternoon my dad's father, my grandfather Sherlock, came to visit me. I was surprised as I had not seen him since the day he moved into dad's house near the factory, I don't even know if he was at dad's funeral. He had his dog with him. As soon as I saw this dog, I remembered the day we went to look through the house Dad bought, pop had already moved in and dad had said, "don't go near or touch pop's dog, and watch the little ones near it". The baby was fine I carried her, and we held the other 2 by the hand. After looking around inside the house dad put the dog indoors away from us, so the kids could roam freely in the yard. The dog was some kind of pit-bull cross, all black; his name was "Nigga" a terrible name. Because of all this, I kept the kids inside this day and didn't invite pop in my house. As I stood talking to pop, I realised he was an unbelievably inconsiderate dog owner. This dog cocked his leg all over my verandah and pop never said a word. Anyhow the reason for his visit was to ask me if I could ask my mother if he could continue to live in the house now dad was gone. There was no way I was going to do that, so I said why don't you just phone her I am sure it would be all right if you talk to her. I don't know if he ever phoned her, but he continued to live in the house rent free as he had always done. Pop said this day he had had a pacemaker put in his heart and he was not well. I really felt uncomfortable talking to him even though he was my grandfather I felt really uneasy, and I could not stop looking at that dog. He had gallons of bright yellow piddle in him, and it was running down my front door and walls as he continuously relieved himself. Big job to wash and remove the smell, after he left! I did not see my pop again!

Pop passed away in Woy Woy Hospital in 1986. We weren't contacted and don't know when the funeral was held. But mum was notified when Pop's Will was read and he had left the house he was living in, dad's house, to dad's only living brother, who happened to be Beverley's father. He had come down from Queensland, been told by whoever had Pop's will he had inherited a house, sold all the furniture, and cleared out the house ready to put it on the market. Unbelievable! Because pop had continued to live there, with no interference paying the electricity bill only, he had taken possession, he thought. There was no-way this house was going on the market without the knowledge of my mother as she paid the rates, and the house was in her name. (This was all done automatically by dads' solicitor as this is what dads old will stated, everything left to my wife). Another family feud I thought, and I had to listen to my mother rant and rave about this silly old fool. But I think Pop did this on purpose, as he knew exactly who owned the house he lived in! Pop had left his car and that awful dog to a friend who had lived close by and eventually my uncle went back to Queensland not happy, but, understanding.

It was the end of another year and my husband's boss took us out for dinner. We were sitting and having drinks after our meal. A woman kept looking in our direction. For a time, I did not know who she was actually looking at. Then she approached me. She asked me if I recognised her, she was familiar, but I didn't know. She said she was my father's secretary for quite a number of years. She said she had seen me at the funeral that is why she was sure of whom I was. As we chatted about if I had kids, where I was living etc., she dropped a bomb shell. For what reason she bought this up, I don't know, maybe she thought I knew, but she said, 'well did your father ever find out, who the man was your mother was having the affair with'! In total shock, I said 'I don't know'! I could not wait to get away from her. All the pieces started finding a place to finally fit. No wonder dad was lashing out with his fists in rage. He must have been so embarrassed and humiliated if his workers were talking about his wife in this way. This had all happened so may years ago I had given up trying to understand and now this one question bought back memories of words that had been yelled and everything started to fall into place. I recalled my mother saying as she was angrily cleaning her shoes one day that she had ruined a perfectly good pair of shoes walking to a man's place who was an employee of dads. She said she had been to give him a piece of her mind for something he had said. All these, little things flashed through my mind, and I did not want these thoughts there.

I would not ever be able to bring myself to tell my mother about this woman, what she said, or ask mum for the truth she would never tell me. I could not even tell her about the small things, dad had talked to me about, such as the plans he had for his retirement, she would say it was not so or I was making things up, she did the same to my husband, if she didn't know about it and it concerned my father it wasn't so. Some kind of denial I suspected because he hadn't talk to her and she was hearing things second-hand.

That night I tossed and turned. No wonder my mother didn't confide in her family about her beatings, she would have had to answer a lot of questions and maybe in answers she may have incriminated herself. Unbelievable! Could this be the true answer to my years of mental torture as I watch my parents abuse each other?

Uncle Norm had continued to come up to the farm after dad's death. He would come alone most of the time to stay the weekend in his caravan. He pottered around the place helping out, where he could. Mum never said much about him being there he was a nice old man. One weekend he arrived with one of his grandsons he was about the same age as my brother. On the Sunday morning that little boy came inside mum's house it was early and he had to wake her. He said he could not wake up his pop. Uncle Norm had died in his sleep. It must have been awful that morning with the police and ambulance there. Mum had to mind that little boy till his father came to pick him up. Mum rang to tell me this had happened but that same week one of my friend's little girl had also passed away and I was unable to attend Uncle Norm's Funeral.

Photo 5. Uncle Norm

The years rushed by. I was as busy as any other mums. Life was good. The 2 older children now at school and on as many weekends as we could manage it, we took camping trips.

I read about how Forster parents were needed in our area, so my husband and I were given all the necessary investigating to be able to have Forster children come to stay at our house. As we were short term foster carers many little ones came and went. It was very hard sometimes when these children left, some we grew very attached too other not so and seeing them go wasn't so difficult. I would be hiding the truth not saying some were really difficult. There were so many reasons for them behaving badly most we were never told about on their arrival. Neglect, sexually abused and beaten, still showing the bruises. Ignorance was a blessing in some of their cases.

We had one little boy who was with us for weeks. He was not walking when he came and didn't talk, but by the time he left we were the only family he had memory of. He called me mum because that's' what he heard, he ran around after my children, they loved him too. But his parents were getting him back and that is the way it was meant to be. The day he left was a most heart-breaking day. As the social worker drove him out the drive he screamed and held his arms out to me. It was a horrible feeling. After that day I didn't have Forster children again. I had never considered feeling that close to a child that was not mine.

Through these times we had opened our home and family life to help some others just a little bit and we did have good memories. Our children shared not only their toys and clothes but their parents' time with these little strangers.

My brother Scot was completing year 12 at High school. Mum could not attend his Graduation celebration, she had a girls' night out for tennis I think, anyway, we attended and sat with my husbands' boss as their youngest was Graduating from the same class. Scot looked so handsome in his black suit and blue bowtie. I was pleased to be there and applauded as he collected his papers. After that night Scot went to Schoolies in Queensland with his friends and had a great holiday. I still have the post-card he sent me from there. He was living it up. He wrote, love this freedom!

Two months later Scot was turning 18. Mum had dad's dress watch cleaned and revamped, to give as a gift to him. There was nothing special about that watch, except that it had belonged to dad, and he had worn it all the time.

Scot bought a car, got a job and would from time-to-time pop in at our house. He was as any other 18-year-old; he had good friends and went out with them on weekends. I also looked forward to his visits when he would tell me about those friends and the girls he liked.

1988. My youngest had started school this year and I had a job between school hour 10am to 2pm each day. Scot liked a girl I was working with and when he could, in his lunch break, he would drive out for a visit and a chat. Of course, it was to see the girl, but I looked forward to this always.

There was one night when Scot visited us at home that I was really worried about his state of mind. He was so upset and stressed because he had had an argument with mum. Fights had happened before, but it was something about this fight that made me worry. He wanted to move out. I didn't think him confiding in me alone, was a good thing. Mum and I did not get along he needed to talk to someone who could maybe see the other side of the disagreement. My husband took Scot to the Pub for a drink. Scot didn't really have a taste for beer or spirits, he was like dad in this way, neither of them drank, but the atmosphere in the pub was always good. Anyway, while they were gone, I did something that wasn't like me, I phoned my sister. I was thinking of sending him there next to talk to her. It was a mistake, she said she did not wish to be involved, she did not want Scot to talk to her about mum, she, said, he would have to sort out his own issues with our mother. I don't know what her real problem was that day. Maybe, it was me calling her as I have said we were not close and didn't talk much. Maybe, she already knew about the argument, mum and she talked all the time. Anyway, Scot would have to make do with my point of view that day. Be it right or wrong. But at least he didn't move out of home.

August came and it was my youngest 6th birthday. Scot dropped in that week he had bought a new car. It was a small Yellow 2 door 4w.d. and he took me and the kids for a drive up the mountain in it to show us how it handled over the rough terrain. He was so proud of that car. He showed me every knob and button and how it all worked. The kids and I showed interest, and I was pleased he had something he really wanted. I remembered that was one of the things his $5,000 was going to buy. I assumed he got a loan to pay the balance.

September 11, 1988. My husband and I had that weekend, painted our daughter's bedroom. It was a pretty shade of pale pink. It was Grand final footy weekend and neither of us are a footy follower, so we finished off the paint work that morning and in the late afternoon put the furniture back in place. That night we put the girls in our double bed as the smell of paint was too strong for them, I thought. We opened the windows to their full extent and slept in their single beds in a room filled with their dolls and a white plastic chain full of their teddies pegged by their ears hung from the ceiling. I was pleased with the way we had decorated our girl's room.

It was about 2am when the phone rang. I was so disorientated my legs were running when my feet hit the floor, I must have been sound asleep. I ran to the kitchen to answer the ringing. As I picked up the receiver, I saw the kitchen clock 2am. I knew the news was not going to be good. But when it was my mother's voice, I felt my knees buckle. She said Scots dead! I was so shocked and started to call my husband, who was well on his way into the kitchen, I could not talk properly I was echoing mum's words. Scots dead! He took the phone, held on to me under his armpit tightly while saying to my mother, we will be right there.

We pulled the 3 kids from the beds, put them in the car and drove to mums. It wasn't till I saw her state, that it hit me, it was really, true. My sister arrived shortly after she was on her own. She had left her husband and kids at home. Mum had already been to identify Scots body. The police came, and picked her up, and then at her insistence dropped her back off alone at her home. The police offered to call family for mum, so she didn't have to be alone, but she said she had no-one! The police left, and I do not know how much later that is when she called us.

Sunrise came, Mum told me, because she thought I was the strong one and I could handle it, (what else would she think, I always hid my emotions) I had to, at 7am, phone everyone to tell them what had happened before they turned on their radios and heard the news as they were releasing Scots name. But before I could do that, I had to know the details, people would ask questions. I wanted to be able to answer.

So, mum proceeded to tell us. At about 10pm Scot and his friend Sean, were coming along the Pacific Hwy, Scot was driving his small 4wd, when a Ford sedan full of drunken young people 6 in all, left the nearby Pub were, they had been celebrating the Grand final footy. They had been travelling over the speed limit came around a sweeping bend too wide drifted on the wrong side of the road and head on into the path of my brother's car. Scot was killed instantly. While his passenger Sean, escaped with only a broken nose, he was trapped in the wreckage for a long time till he was finally cut free. A terrible thing for anybody! With this in my mind I had to make those phone calls. I remember asking some people I phoned to lighten my burden by making some calls on my behalf.

Before going home that day, I asked my mother, a question that had been troubling me. What was Scot doing out on a Sunday night so late when he had to go to work the next morning. I was shocked to hear the story she was about to tell, and I know she would, if not so heartbroken, never have answered my question.

That day Scot had stopped at a petrol station, and he had put fuel in his car. When, he went to pay for that petrol he could not find any money in his pockets or wallet, so he handed the service station owner his watch, the one that use to belong to our father, the one that he was given for his 18th birthday, as security while he drove home to get money to pay. When he arrived home, he told mum he was just back to get something and was going again, he would be back for tea. I don't know exactly why or how it came about mum never really said, but he told mum about the watch at the service station. Our mother being as she is made a big deal out of it; they had an argument and Scot left in a huff and must have decided not to return home for tea and to stay out late. Mum was devastated that their last words were angry ones. Not one of us could think of any words of comfort for her. We just let it be. My personal thoughts were, the watch was his, he could do as he liked with it. When my husband and I discussed it later he told me he would have done the same thing he said it is what you do leave something of value to show good faith and that you will return.

Two days later mum rang. She asked if I could go to the wreckage of Scots car and pick-up his toolbox and his music tapes. I also was asked to pick-up

Scots belongings at the police station. My husband came with me to do this. On the way home I nursed my brother's things. While holding the last things he had on him I found myself looking through his wallet. He had the usual contents in there, a few coins, his driver's licence, phone numbers on pieces of paper. As I made a pile of these things in my lap, I discovered something that bought me undone. In the back envelope part of his wallet amongst some pieces of paper was a $20 note. Was it there all the time? I worried, had he not remembering he put this there cost him his life? Or did he get this extra money when he returned home? I will never know! I didn't tell anyone else that money was there my husband and I have kept it secret. It is too heartbreaking, the thoughts that run through your mind. The what if's, the why's, I stopped myself thinking about all this.

Auntie Jean and Uncle Frank were the first to arrive and were there for mum again.

We went to view Scot's body. Even though mum had already seen him, we were all there together including auntie Jean and uncle Frank. It was a small room at the back of the hospital. My brother lay behind a glass window. We were not able to touch him. He was totally covered with a white sheet and had a large bandage over his head, but it was clear to see it was really him. I cannot, explain my emotions, I wanted to scream but everyone else stood so quietly, I held it back. I could not believe I was there looking at my brother's lifeless body he was so young, and he was dead through no fault of his own. Killed by a drunk driver!

The mortician gave my mother a small bag with the remainder of Scot's possessions mainly, his clothes. On the way home in the car mum opened the bag and began to take out his things and there must have been the watch because I heard her say, 'now what am I going to do with this watch?' Without even turning my head to look at her in the back seat I said, it can be buried with him for all I care, no-one wants it! Without hesitation, mum said O.K! I'll give it to the funeral director. I was shocked I had actually said something my mother agreed with and on the morning of the funeral the watch was placed on my brother arm, and he was buried next to our father.

I had many a day where I battled endlessly with my emotions. I had kept the kids out of school too long and after a phone conversation with one of their teachers who implied I was using my brother's death as an excuse for my children not getting on with things, I tried to get back into the swing of our day to day lives, but it was hard to come around from all the shock and I had not finished crying. I knew I had to get a grip for my family's sake. I went back to work that helped. I was so busy there my mind would not let me think of anything but the job at hand and after months I began to feel normal again.

Mum needed to discuss something with us all. so, we went to the farm again. As we sat around her kitchen bench, she explained she had to write a new Will. I did not think losing a child would warrant making a new Will, but you see as mum explained after dad's death, she had left everything she had from dads Will to Scot.

I was amazed, she had 3 children, but she was telling us she had left all she had to leave to one. I didn't care, because it was Scot, but to tell us straight out that she thought more of one of her children than she did of others made me feel unimportant and I thought, I do not need to know any of this. Why didn't she just make her will and leave us out of the preparation, she had managed before to do this, and we had been none the wiser of her previous decision. I didn't know what I was doing there. About then I remember Scot telling me dad had died before signing his new Will. Maybe dad had wanted it this way. This did not sound like dad but, maybe! So, I thought I would ask mum in front of my sister, her husband, and my husband if dad had made a new Will. So, I did! In a bit of shock, she said yes, he had, and I destroyed it and none of you will ever know what was written in it! Well, that answered that question. After that I just said, simply because you wanted my input, anything you think I am entitled too, and I die before you, please leave it in equal shares to my three children.

What an awful experience, I wanted to go home, and we did.

Christmas was coming up and I had children who believed in Santa so I had to force myself to do all the things I would have normally delighted in. It all seemed like a chore this year. One of my aunts had invited us to her home to celebrate Christmas day with them. She had 5 children who were married with children of their own, but as we had tea on Christmas night with my family, well now mum,

I had to check with her that this arrangement was still good. Mum said, tea that night as usual would be fine, so I went ahead with my arrangement. We went to my aunts at about 11am Christmas morning after the kids had opened their presents and had time to play with them while eating their breakfast. The day was great, we all sat around this big, long table on the verandah which was closed in with fly screening and decorated with coloured streamers. They had a real Spruce tree in a pot my children had never seen one of those before as we always had an artificial tree. My husband drank and enjoyed the company of my cousins and the kids all played together in the yard. That afternoon my aunts husband got out the tractor and trailer, the kids all piled on and they went all over their farmyard. The time was getting on and I had to think of gathering everyone up and setting off to mums for tea. It wasn't far away about 20 minutes' drive, but we had to get going.

We arrived at mums about 4.30-5pm, she was standing at the sink preparing the food. I walked over to say Merry Christmas and what do you want me to help with, when, she let loose on me. Where have you been? You would think that you would want to be here with me the first Christmas without Scot? You are a selfish and thoughtless girl! I was drawn back, but not surprised, I knew I did nothing right in her eyes it was a normal thing for her to lash out at me, so I simply said I am not the only person in my family, and I was considering my husband and children today they are important to me also! We have tried to make the most of the day too! It is only early. We have the rest of the night! But that was not good enough for her she continued to yell at me. Then my sister who had been there with her for a few hours started to join in, echoing mum's words. I was starting to feel I was in the wrong as they both threw their critisms at me. Then from the doorway my husband yelled. Shut-up! They did, and he then continued with, I have been listening to you criticise and put my wife down since I came into this family, and I have had enough. It is Christmas day! He then asked the kids to get back into the car. He then looked at me and said you to. We have had enough! There were a few other things he said but those words of defence on my behalf from my normally quiet husband are really all I took notice of. I was so grateful he had walked in and heard enough to make a snap decision on getting out of there. I was torn on the way home as to whether I should have been there all day with a mother who was not of a loving nature toward me, but after all she was still my mother and she was suffering the loss of my brother. Then I thought how my sister had been there with her and how she could have thought of something to say to calm her down a little, instead she joined in and had verbally attacked me too. My husband for the first time had let me know how fed-up he was with my family. He said if your mother wanted us to spend the day with her, she had a right to tell you when you phoned to ask what time she wanted us to come up here. You don't deserve to be treated like that, she can't blame you for her not speaking-up, and she is quick to tell you what she wants of you any other time. My husband noticed more than I thought he did even though he had said little over the years he had taken a lot in. I appreciated him. He was my soulmate, my rock.

I can't remember how long it was before mum and I spoke again. But I remember there were bush fires in her area and all the houses had to be evacuated including my mothers. We drove up in the truck and helped mum gather her important and valuable possessions and took her to our house where she stayed for a few days till the fire danger had passed. We didn't ever talk about that Christmas afternoon, but mum decided each Christmas thereafter, she would do her own thing and she does. It must have been an eyeopener for my mother spending those few days with us in our home. My children with their outspoken attitudes, she always said kids should be seen and not heard, well our kids were both!

Mum went on several over-seas' holidays through the next few years, and she sold the old house pop use to live in and eventually she sold the farm too. She bought a house close to where she spent most of her time, playing tennis and squash.

On one occasion when mum visited, our dog Raz, (my dad got him for the kids), ran to greet her at the gate, so he didn't jump on her see gave him a slap across the snout. We didn't see this, but, as we walked her out after her visit there was a tooth on the path. My husband picked it up and said, big tooth! My mother said it could be the dogs, I gave him a back hander when I got here. Yes, it was poor Raz's, a simple sit would have done it, but she was always so physical, and lashed out!

As My husband and I raised our children we were believers in allowing them to express their feeling so if there were any signs of hostility towards each other that looked like they were going on for too long we would have what I called a round table discussion. I did not want my children to clam-up and become moody individuals that were too afraid to show their true self in our family unit. This was never to judge only to help keep our lines of communication open through our busy lives so nothing important escaped undealt with. At these round table meetings, we aired our grievances with each other and cleared our consensus and tried to help resolve any really disturbing issues that they may have on their minds, their groups of friends, nights out, drugs, alcohol, and sex when they were older. We never pried, we never had to. They just talked openly.

The years went passed so quickly. Tap classes, Gymnastics, Softball, swimming lessons, tuition, before I knew it my children grew-up, graduated from their schools then their Tech courses, got their drivers licences, good jobs, all three were independent, socially acceptable wonderful people, each in their own way and now they have partners to share their lives with. But leading up to this end result I was a worrier and had sleepless nights. I was always prepared for the worst. I think I wanted everything to be too perfect. I was once told by a friend I wanted my family to be like the Brady Bunch, every problem found and solved within an half'n'hour episode. Maybe that was right. But I looked on my position as a mother and wife as a serious job.

We wanted to have the kind of home that the kids could bring their friends into and have parties. I think we achieved this as the kids' friends we still see but these days it is their engagements, weddings, and baby's christenings.

But what energy I wasted through their teenage years. I worried when they were out at night and cried if they were not home on time. I yelled at them. I worried and cried when they drove their cars and motor bikes. I did not realise that to worry is a waste of energy and it makes no difference to any outcome. I worried myself sick. I ended up at the doctor. What I thought my problem was, frightened me. Some kind of mental issues I thought. Sometimes, I could not bring myself to leave the house. I would not even go to the letter box some days. Knowing I had a problem,

I decided again to seek some kind of counselling. I opened up again as I had all those years ago under different circumstance, when my kids were small. I came to understand myself and move on. I had never really dealt with my father's sudden death. My children were so small I had no time to really grieve. Then my brother's death, so tragic, killed by a drunk driver. The years I had witnessed my parent's abuse each other and my mind was so fill of this as I puzzled over the reasons why for years. All these tragedy's the less than normal childhood. When I talked about all these events, there was a lot to deal with and it was not too late. How do other people cope with life's tragedies, surely my life could not have been that far outside of what would be referred to as the usual.

The diagnosis was P.T.S.D (post-traumatic stress disorder) panic attacks and depression.

As I came to terms with the fact that what was wrong with me had a name and that medication would help right my chemical imbalance, I really was thankful I was able to be helped.

So many years of being crushed down and not allowed to show emotions or standing up for myself, fight back with words I kept everything inside.

2007 We moved to the country, a small acre. We had decided to move after coming here for the past 30 years camping and for weekends because we liked the town and the people here. Not that our friends on the coast were less than important to us, we just loved this area. We did not hesitate to leave our kids living 2 ½ hours' drive away they all had these good jobs, and their lives were full. It was a time for us, my husband and I to enjoy a tree change, as they say!

I had another one of those phone calls. Someone had died. This time it was my sister's youngest child. She had been coming home from a party about 3am on a push bike, no helmet, no lights. Anyway, a fisherman on his way home towing his boat, didn't realise it but he had hit her. She died before the ambulance arrived. Such tragic news! I did not know till then my sister's marriage had broken down her husband had a new partner and she and her daughter had been living in a unit/flat in one of the beach areas in Sydney.

I phoned my mother and spoke to my sister whom I had not seen for years. I had trouble knowing what to say. I would not have had the right words for anyone. What can be said! I am sorry to hear your sad news and I hope….. ! I don't know exactly what I said.

I know I had a feeling of guilt, all that was running through my head was I am so glad that this did not happen to me, and I needed to hear the sound of my own children's voices.

I sent flowers to the funeral, but I was not going to attend. I was estranged from my sister and mother I knew nothing of my sister's life or her children. I was not under these circumstances going to reunite with them. I would not want me there. I am an outsider now having no contact for about 16 years makes that so. I didn't know if I wanted to reunite with both of them together under any circumstances. This was not a punishment toward them I was worried for my own state of mind and what I could handle. I was still on my meds, but my fear was, how I handled this was going to affect not only me but reflect on my children and husband. I couldn't explain it, I know they were the family I was born into, but I was afraid of what they could do to my stability. I had kept going back all those years before only to be made feel bad about myself. I had no emotional connection with them that was long gone. I was sad for my sister's loss, but only the same kind of sadness I would feel for anyone who had lost their child.

The following week I contacted my mother I thought I would ask how she and my sister were coping. I could not entirely ignore the sad situation they were going through. I would have liked to, but it played on my mind to make this call. We were disconnected at first, I thought, so I tried again. My mother said, 'don't you get a hint I don't want to talk to you!' I said that's fine I call back later. She said, 'I never want to talk to you!' She said that I had done myself no favours not attending this funeral that people did not like me, and I now would have no friends. Again, my mother told me where I stood, and I again moved on and put it out of my mind.

Our eldest daughter was engaged, and we were planning the wedding. It was so exciting and naturally we wanted everything perfect. I knew she would have my mother on the guest list I would not have expected her to leave her out, so I thought I would write my mother a letter. I did not want my husband and kids to be worried she was going to show up cranky and nasty toward me in front of guest. They had let me know they had these uneasy feeling she might be less than happy to see and be with me. I had become quite comfortable now in my 50's with the fact my mother disliked me and thought I made wrong decisions she had let me know what a disappointment as a daughter I was to her. But I preferred on this day she didn't let loose with all the insults and critisms. I simply said in this letter, I am who I am. I don't have any issues with you and on the day, you are seated next to me and for those few hours could you just be my mother. (I really meant a caring mother toward me, but she would have taken that as an insult, and it would not have helped).

She wrote back, I would rather not come if I had to do as you tell me! She also wrote all the usual stuff she had said so many times before. It hurt; it was meant to!

But my mother came to the wedding of course!

Months before the wedding day there was a wedding dress to select out of the millions out there. The one exactly right! Unlike many girls, I though, she insisted that her father come and help with this decision along with myself and her sister. She had remembered from when she was a little girl and her father had told her when she married, he would take her to a bridal shop in the city. He sat in a great big high backed red velvet chair in a Bridal

Shop in the out skirts of Sydney watching on as she paraded dress after dress. Then there it was the most perfect off-white hand beaded dress. It was obvious she loved it. Without hesitating her father said, "I'm paying the deposit!" We had the best day! (Before the youngest daughter married, we did it all again & also with our daughter-in-law to be!)

Then another surprise my daughters had planned a trip to Thailand. It was a girls' only shopping holiday and I was invited to go with them. We shopped, walked with the Tigers, saw the Bridge on the river Kwai, Temples and exhausted ourselves day after day. The only time my daughters complained to me was because each morning I get up early and first thing I do is to have my cup of Coffee, unfortunately the kettle in our suite sounded more like a freight train than a kettle so I disturbed them every morning. But that even though annoying, they could live with.

Somewhere along the way, my husband's parents had to sell their family home, in Sydney. Because they were at various stages of health, staying in the city meant they would have been put in separate facilities and after 60 years of marriage that was not going to happen. So, to stay together, they had to move out of the city. This was a difficult decision, these city folk had to move to the country, to where my husband's older brother lives, to a newly completed retirement village in the hospital grounds, 10 minutes away from family. This was a rollercoaster ride for everyone! A large home with the possessions of a lifetime had to be dealt with. The four of us, (which consisting of two brothers and their wives) had to sort and dispose of everything. Heartbreaking for this old couple! Trucked all their furniture, but it did not fit in the new unit, we did tell them, but this they had to realise for themselves. Got rid of it all and bought new furniture. Then back to the city for a final complete clean and lock the door for the last time! Then one after the other they passed away, him first aged 90years, then a few years later, her aged 92years. Back we were again cleaning out another home for them. My husband's family was so far apart from mine, I never felt anything but an important and needed family member and love from this old couple.

The Wedding Day was here I was so excited and busy through the week I really had no time to think of anything other than my daughter the bride, 3 bridesmaids (her sister and two girlfriends), my son and his girlfriend who were all staying here and of course the father of the bride, my husband. The videographer and the photographer all these people were busily rushing around the house. Just wonderful it was.

She had known exactly how she wanted their wedding day. The reception venue a very big old timber shearing shed filled with the rustic charms of years past. Even though they had made their home on the coast and had been together 7 years, (to that day), she had always wanted to go off to her wedding from our family home and after seeing this venue it all started to be planned. My daughter had thought of everything even a bus for the guests who were staying in town at the motel, so they had no problems finding the wedding venue. The guests wanting to drive simply followed the bus. The remainder of the guest all her young friends were at the guest house on the property where she and her new husband were spending the night. They intended to party on after the reception and through the night.

To get there ourselves my son drove one car with myself and the three bridesmaids, his girlfriend drove the other car with the bride, and her father.

On their arrival at the property 5ks away where the events of the day were taking place, a shiny old black buggy drawn by a big, beautiful horse was waiting there in a grassy valley just far enough away for the guests not to see the bride and bridesmaids organising themselves for the big arrival. The driver of the buggy was a little old man dressed up in a suit with a top hat. Perfect! In the garden under the shade of towering trees waited her husband–to-be, family and guests for her expectedly late arrival

The whole event went off wonderfully but was over in the blink of an eye. My mother sat next to me through the reception and appeared to enjoy the entire day.

The next morning Sunday we had a big breakfast for all who wanted to join in, mostly everyone who had stayed overnight were there. The wedding presents were opened and as lunch time drew near everyone started to set off for their trips home.

That afternoon I settled my 91-year-old mother-in-law into her room. (This was the last time we were to have her stay). She had travelled with her son my husband's brother and his wife to attend the wedding and had been staying in town at the motel with the other guests. That day they had to return home but because of her age and the long trip back we had decided if she stayed with us for a few days after the wedding it would be a good opportunity for her to spend time with us and break the trip up over a week. We would take her home when she was ready to travel. I decided I would phone my mother at the motel; I thought maybe she would come over as she had not attended the breakfast that morning.

To my surprise she had checked out that morning. While waiting out the time it would take her friends to drive her home I prepare tea, help my mother-in-law take her hearing aids out (they use to make her ears sore), shower, take her meds and get ready for bed and because she was now reading a book, I phoned my mother at her home. She was not happy to hear my voice and let loose with the usual insults. Unfortunately for me I had in her eyes given her more reasons to express her dislike for me. My mother asked to be put on the speaker phone so my husband could hear what a horrid person I was.

First, she started with how she had to catch the bus with the other guest she had wanted to be picked-up in person by one of us. But the bus was there so we didn't have to go into town to pick-up anyone. Then she rambled on about not being there for the breakfast and she had missed out. Why didn't your friend drive you I asked, she said she never asked them too, because they wanted to set off early for home! Then she said she had been quite happily sitting talking to another elderly lady at the wedding when that lady's' son came over excused himself and said, he was taking his mother to sit with him and their family as they didn't spend enough time with her and they wanted to make the most of her while they had her! Why would he do that she said, I was left sitting on my own. That elderly lady was my new son-in-law's grandmother! My husband said to me "don't even try to make sense of anything she says or reply, it would be useless she would never understand." Mum, preceded again to repeat her nasty words to me! Why did you get the happy life, why did you get the good husband, you don't deserve it! I hope something happens to one of yours, so you know how your sister and I feel! OMG! Who would even think such a thing?... I eventually said goodbye and hung up the phone. My mother-in-law reading in the lounge room, I had forgotten about, she called out and said she was ready for bed. My husband helping, got her walking frame and as we followed her shuffling down the hall, she said your mother is a bit queer, isn't she!

She wasn't as deaf as we thought. I don't know how much she heard but it must have been enough. Feeling embarrassed I never spoke!

Only a couple of years had passed since then and I have contacted my mother trying to talk to her as we will be having other wedding in the next few years, I wanted her to get over her issues with me. Some kind of truce so we could enjoy these special events, but it was like talking to a brick wall. As I tried to open up to her telling her I had had counselling to help me, she butted in and told me I had a normal childhood. I swore into the phone at her. I had never been disrespectful or used bad language at my mother before, that is how frustrated I was with her comment. She said, she wished she were face to face with me so she could hit me. Resorting to violence was her way, but it solved nothing!

After that day, my contact with my mother has been, Mother's Day, Christmas day, birthdays, family news, births, and deaths just a few times a year I will call her, or she will call me. That is about it, and she is always civil to me during those short conversations.

These past years has bought so many changes to our lives and I would not have liked to live these years any other way. We want to continue to help our adult kids out where possible as do many parents these days. Because our children liked this area so much and were thinking about moving here, we welcomed them back home if that is where they wanted to be, to help them achieve their dreams earlier. Our son and his girlfriend moved in here to live with us short term after both securing new jobs here and they built their new home, while living on our property. Our eldest daughter and her husband sold their home on the coast and went overseas for 6 months on their belated honeymoon. After they returned our son-in-law moved in here with us, started work while our daughter went back to her old job which was waiting for her on the coast she moved in with her sister during this time. Then 6 months later they found a property here about 20 minutes' drive, from our home. Our oldest daughter applied for a new job quit her old job and they moved into their new home. Our youngest daughter says she would never move from the coast she says she could never leave her job there. But her partner who had steady work here also lived with us and goes home weekends. He was with us about 18 months. This has all worked. They saved money settled into a new area and we all supported each other and helped. Eventually our youngest daughter eventually took the step and moved here too!

Dec 2009 my mother was about to celebrate her 80th birthday! I suggested to my husband and children who had no idea how old she was how about we meet Nana for lunch. Do something and let her know we remembered she was turning 80. It is a 2½ hour trip and my eldest daughter, and her husband would be there on the coast anyway for a wedding, so she rang her nana and asked if she wanted to do lunch before they headed home. My mother said yes, and they arranged a time to pick her up, 12 o'clock Sunday. The 6 of us met at the restaurant in the Ocean Beach Hotel. There was a bunch of yellow roses the kids had bought for her and also some small presents these things were in the centre of the table. We were looking at the menu when my daughter and her husband arrived with mum. My mother stopped at the entrance to the restaurant looked over at our table and we waved hello to her. She looked for a moment then said I do not want to stay, to my eldest daughter, who turned looked at us and shrugged her shoulders. The next thing my mother started to walk away. With that my daughters followed her to ask, 'what was the problem'! They had just disappeared out of sight when I decided to see for myself. I hurried around the corner. They were standing at the pedestrian crossing. I said "Mum, aren't you going to come in and have lunch with us"? I don't want to eat with you she barked. You have not been a daughter to me! Why would you do this! She asked. Cause you are turning 80 and we wanted to let you know we remembered! I tried to stay calm and said, come on in we all want to celebrate your birthday tomorrow! She added, "You had your chance, she said when your sister's daughter died you had your chance with me!" I said, 'I'm not interested in the past!' We would like you to stay! She continued with her rambling. As I stood listening to her insults, I noticed she was shaking with rage. Well, I am assuming that is why she was shaking! Suddenly I found myself filling with anger toward her as I listened to her insult me again and again Infront of my daughters. My mind wander to the fact we were all there, we had unselfishly given up our day, travelled 2 ½ hours for her and she was so nasty. I could not believe she was going to treat my whole family as if their feelings didn't count because she didn't like decisions I had made in the past! Suddenly I blurted out at her I am 55 years old I am not going to be spoken to like that anymore, look at you shake. Its ok, I looked at my daughters and said, "Its ok to take her home!" As I turned my back to walk away my mother started yelling out at me, come back, I'm not finished with you! I just kept walking. 'Oh! Yes, you are I thought.' Back inside the restaurant the boys, daughter-in-law to be, and husband sat waiting unaware of what had been said outside. I had to say something, but my girls would no doubt tell what happened. So, I simply said, she's not staying to eat and it's because of me! There were comments made but the main one was she must be mad! I wasn't sure if that meant she must be mad at me! Or she must be mad as in crazy! I didn't ask. When my youngest daughter returned, she was crying. I consoled her. She looked at me and asked, 'how can you not cry all those terrible things she said to you!" I don't know I answered maybe I have cried all I can over the years. Anyway, I have heard it all before. Not one of us had the stomach for a meal we all just left and went home. The waitresses must have thought us weird, first we were planning our meal then we were gone!

On the trip home my husband said to me. That's it now, you are not going to put yourself in that position again with her. I seemed fine though, it wasn't till halfway through the week that it finally hit me. How were things going to unfold in the years to come with 2 more weddings coming up in the future! Would the kids even bother to include her after she has now shown them their feelings mean nothing to her! She was so intent in making me look bad in the eyes of my family she had not considered how she would be remembered by them. She is their Nana and that she should have remembered! Nanas are supposed to be loving old ladies that grandchildren want to be with. My children and their partners that day deserved more.

My son married, but it was a small wedding in Fiji, my mother was not invited. Too old to fly they said. My youngest daughter married soon after, close to where my mother lives so she attended that wedding and sat at our table. This wedding was a very big wedding, lots of noise and with their many friends partying and dancing, so my mother was pretty quiet. We organised a lift home for her so she would have nothing to complain about!

She, now, says she regrets the day she would not eat with my family.!

We only have Christmas Day all together every 2nd year as the alternate years my children go to their in-laws. About 8 years back I said to my family, should we invite my mother here to spend Christmas with us. The answer was really, don't do it to yourself, so it never happened. It saddens me, she has missed out on seeing and being involved in many of my family's special times together.

The way I see it is I have lived my married life honestly, fully and priorities the things that to me are the most important. My decisions through this time whether they be right or wrong in other eyes are beside the point to me. I will always guard myself against those individuals who make life difficult. I will want to put them into the background.

Who needs them! Especially those who only see your short comings!

Although I saw my father do unspeakable things when I was a child! I forgave him and never looked back at my decision to do this! Even though my mother was angry about it!

I was treated cruelly growing up in an unloving home!

I married the first time the wrong person for the wrong reasons! But the second time I got it right!

Suffered the loose of dad and Scot! I grieved after I was shown how!

I learnt things about my mother that I never want to confront her with! My choice!

I continually put myself in the position of allowing her to tell me what a dreadful daughter and person she thought I was. Wrongly thinking because she was my mother, she had the right and she thought she had the right because she was my mother.

I suffered anxiety attacks, depression and tortured dreams!

Honesty and openness are important! Without this life can go into a dark place.

Through this emotional roller-coaster of my life, I have tried not to pass my emotional crippling memories on to my children through verbal, or physical abuse. Until I wrote this down, they had not much knowledge of my parents. I just thought it may have been a burden they could live without knowing the disturbing parts of my life. Also, they never knew my father so I never wanted them in their young years to judge him for what he had done because I know I would try to defend his memory as my parents were as bad as each other with physical violence, I would feel compelled to tell them what that employee of my father said about my mother, and she was a part of their young lives. Best to keep certain subjects till mature years.

October 2023. As for my mother she still lives on her own in the same house she bought after selling the farm. She is 94 this year.

My mother is blind, Macular Degenerate Disease, so she depends on carers to help her day to day. Over the past years if my children have been in her area, they will visit taking their children with them, for her to hold them as babies, and now to chat too.

This is their choice as I have neither encouraged nor discouraged them from making this choice to know her. They only see their Nana nothing else! No horrible memories. Only the days she use to yell at me when they were young & the day, she would not join us for Lunch.

Now in my late 60's as I go about my daily life my mind wonders, as I think about what my young life dealt me and now the happiness and the many reasons, I am grateful for my husband. The unconditional love we show each other. I am grateful for our children and the way they have grown to be the socially acceptable people they are. They have made me feel important, complete and my life, worthwhile. I have everything I need.

Now with grandchildren to spend time with and watch them grow, life is amazing and until I die, I am not missing a single moment of the rest!

For the past 10 or more years our whole family have lived close by. Close enough so 3 of my Grandchildren walk to visit us, it is incredibly special!!!!

A happy, healthy, loving family is all I ever dreamt of!

www.ingramcontent.com/pod-product-compliance
Lightning Source LLC
LaVergne TN
LVHW040106080526
838202LV00045B/3793